INSPIRATION

THOUGHTS AND QUOTATIONS FOR EVERY DAY

summersdale

INSPIRATION

Summersdale Publishers Ltd
46 West Street
Chichester
West Sussex
PO19 1RP
UK

www.summersdale.com

Printed and bound in the Czech Republic

ISBN: 978-1-78685-240-3

Substantial discounts on bulk quantities of Summersdale books are available to corporations, professional associations and other organisations. For details contact general enquiries: telephone: +44 (0) 1243 771107 or email: enquiries@summersdale.com.

To Ci

From Mom

25/12/2018

IF YOU KNOW YOUR ENEMY AND KNOW YOURSELF, YOU WILL NOT BE IMPERILLED IN A HUNDRED BATTLES.

Sun Tzu

The greater the
OBSTACLE,
the more glory in
OVERCOMING IT.

Molière

Man's
greatness lies in his
power of thought.

Blaise Pascal

Far away there in
the sunshine are my
highest aspirations...
I can look up and see
their beauty, believe
in them, and try
to follow where
they lead.

Louisa May Alcott

IF WE WAIT
FOR THE
MOMENT
WHEN
EVERYTHING,
ABSOLUTELY
EVERYTHING
IS READY,
WE SHALL
NEVER
BEGIN.

Ivan Turgenev

First say to yourself what you would be; and then do what you have to do.

Epictetus

Fall seven times,
stand up eight.

Japanese proverb

How wonderful it is that nobody need wait a single moment before starting to improve the world.

Anne Frank

SOME RUN SWIFTLY; SOME CREEP PAINFULLY; ALL WHO KEEP ON WILL REACH THE GOAL.

Piyadassi Thera

Few things are impossible to diligence and skill. Great works are performed not by strength, but by perseverance.

Samuel Johnson

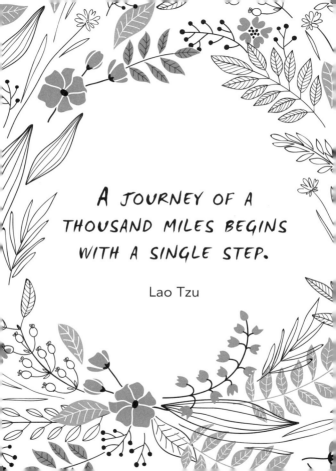

A JOURNEY OF A
THOUSAND MILES BEGINS
WITH A SINGLE STEP.

Lao Tzu

There is no chance,
no destiny, no fate,
Can circumvent or
hinder or control
The firm resolve of
a determined soul.

Ella Wheeler Wilcox

In order to succeed
we must first believe
that we can.

Nikos Kazantzakis

SHOOT FOR THE
MOON. EVEN IF YOU
MISS, YOU'LL LAND
AMONG THE STARS.

Les Brown

The future
belongs to those
who believe in
the beauty of
their dreams.

Eleanor Roosevelt

CONSTANT PRACTICE GIVEN TO ONE MATTER OFTEN CONQUERS BOTH GENIUS AND ART.

Marcus Tullius Cicero

Life shrinks or
expands in proportion
to one's courage.

Anaïs Nin

A CERTAIN AMOUNT OF OPPOSITION IS A GREAT HELP TO A MAN. KITES RISE AGAINST AND NOT WITH THE WIND.

John Neal

A DIAMOND
WITH A FLAW IS
WORTH MORE
THAN A PEBBLE
WITHOUT
IMPERFECTIONS.

Chinese proverb

ATTEMPT THE
IMPOSSIBLE IN ORDER TO
IMPROVE YOUR WORK.

Bette Davis

It is right to be
CONTENTED
with what we have,
but never with
WHAT WE ARE.

James Mackintosh

BETTER THAN A
HUNDRED YEARS
OF IDLENESS
IS ONE DAY
SPENT IN
DETERMINATION.

The Dhammapada

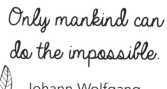

Only mankind can
do the impossible.

Johann Wolfgang
von Goethe

Satisfaction lies in **THE EFFORT,** *not in the attainment. Full effort is* **FULL VICTORY.**

Mahatma Gandhi

THERE IS NO IMPOSSIBILITY TO HIM WHO STANDS PREPARED TO CONQUER EVERY HAZARD.

Sarah J. Hale

Life is a progress,
and not a station.

Ralph Waldo Emerson

Fear is only
as deep as the
mind allows.

Japanese proverb

Only those who have
the patience to
do simple things
perfectly will
acquire the skill
to do difficult
things easily.

Friedrich von Schiller

The people who get on in this world… look for the circumstances they want, and, if they can't find them, make them.

George Bernard Shaw

The time is
always right to do
what is right.

Martin Luther King Jr

REGRET FOR WASTED TIME IS MORE WASTED TIME.

Mason Cooley

IF YOU HAVE AN HOUR, WILL YOU NOT IMPROVE THAT HOUR, INSTEAD OF IDLING IT AWAY?

Lord Chesterfield

I see my path, but I
don't know where it
leads. Not knowing
where I'm going is
what inspires me to
travel it.

Rosalia de Castro

NOTHING CAN STOP THE MAN WITH THE RIGHT MENTAL ATTITUDE FROM ACHIEVING HIS GOAL.

Thomas Jefferson

The way to gain a
GOOD REPUTATION
is to endeavour to be
what you
DESIRE TO APPEAR.

Socrates

All great
achievements
require time.

Maya Angelou

THE ONLY JOURNEY
IS THE ONE WITHIN.

Rainer Maria Rilke

NOTHING GREAT

in the world has been

accomplished without

PASSION.

G. W. F. Hegel

Nothing is a
waste of time
if you use the
experience wisely.

Auguste Rodin

If we all did
the things we
are capable of
doing, we would
literally astound
ourselves.

Thomas Edison

You must first be who
you really are, then
do what you need to
do, in order to have
what you want.

Margaret Young

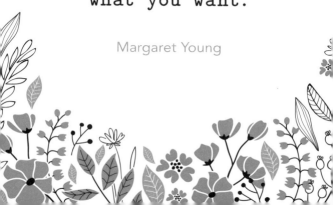

GO CONFIDENTLY IN THE DIRECTION OF YOUR DREAMS. LIVE THE LIFE YOU HAVE IMAGINED.

Henry David Thoreau

Do not follow where
the path may lead.
Go instead where
there is no path
and leave a trail.

Harold R. McAlindon

IT IS HARD TO FAIL,
BUT IT IS WORSE
NEVER TO HAVE TRIED
TO SUCCEED.

Theodore Roosevelt

OUR GREATEST
GLORY CONSISTS
NOT IN NEVER
FALLING, BUT IN
RISING EVERY
TIME WE FALL.

Oliver Goldsmith

ALWAYS BE
READY TO
SPEAK YOUR
MIND, AND A
BASE MAN WILL
AVOID YOU.

William Blake

We must have
PERSEVERANCE
and above all
CONFIDENCE
in ourselves.

Marie Curie

There is no
failure except in no
longer trying.

Elbert Hubbard

To be yourself in
a world that is
constantly trying to
make you something
else is the greatest
accomplishment.

Ralph Waldo Emerson

Whatever you do, do it with all your might.

Marcus Tullius Cicero

THE WAY TO GET
STARTED IS TO
QUIT TALKING AND
BEGIN DOING.

Walt Disney

*Do what you feel
in your heart
to be right.*

Eleanor Roosevelt

OBSTACLES ARE THOSE FRIGHTFUL THINGS YOU SEE WHEN YOU TAKE YOUR EYES OFF THE GOAL.

Henry Ford

SMALL OPPORTUNITIES ARE OFTEN THE BEGINNING OF GREAT ENTERPRISES.

Demosthenes

Unless a man
undertakes more than
he possibly can do,
he will never do all
that he can.

Henry Drummond

COURAGE IS RESISTANCE TO FEAR, MASTERY OF FEAR — NOT ABSENCE OF FEAR.

Mark Twain

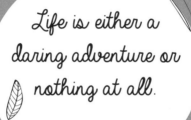

Life is either a daring adventure or nothing at all.

Helen Keller

A WISE MAN WILL MAKE
MORE OPPORTUNITIES
THAN HE FINDS.

Francis Bacon

THE QUESTION SHOULD BE, IS IT WORTH TRYING TO DO, NOT CAN IT BE DONE.

Allard K. Lowenstein

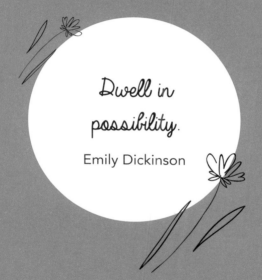

Dwell in possibility.

Emily Dickinson

When it is obvious
that the goals
cannot be reached,
don't adjust the
goals, adjust the
action steps.

Confucius

To climb steep
hills requires a slow
pace at first.

William Shakespeare

Talents are best
nurtured in solitude,
but character is best
formed in the stormy
billows of the world.

Johann Wolfgang von Goethe

THE FIRST MAN GETS THE OYSTER, THE SECOND MAN GETS THE SHELL.

Andrew Carnegie

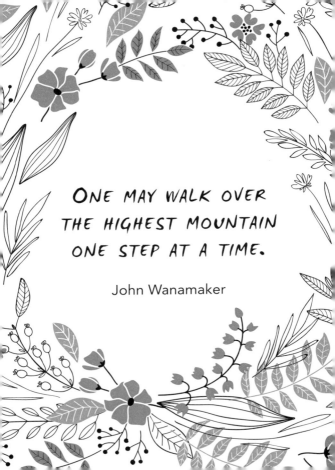

ONE MAY WALK OVER
THE HIGHEST MOUNTAIN
ONE STEP AT A TIME.

John Wanamaker

We are what we
repeatedly do.
EXCELLENCE,
therefore, is not
an act, but
A HABIT.

Aristotle

We reform others

UNCONSCIOUSLY

when we walk

UPRIGHTLY.

Anne Sophie Swetchine

To know oneself,
one should
assert oneself.

Albert Camus

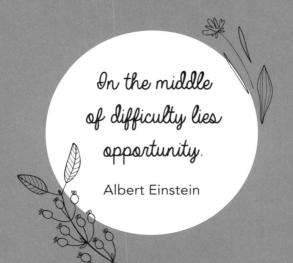

In the middle
of difficulty lies
opportunity.

Albert Einstein

If you have built castles in the air, your work need not be lost; that is where they should be. Now put the foundations under them.

Henry David Thoreau

THE POWER OF IMAGINATION MAKES US INFINITE.

John Muir

EVERYTHING HAS A SMALL BEGINNING.

Marcus Tullius Cicero

IF YOU DO NOT HOPE, YOU WILL NOT FIND WHAT IS BEYOND YOUR HOPES.

St Clement of Alexandra

We are all inventors,
each sailing out
on a voyage of
discovery… The world
is all gates,
all opportunities.

Ralph Waldo Emerson

OPPORTUNITY DOES
NOT KNOCK, IT
PRESENTS ITSELF
WHEN YOU BEAT
DOWN THE DOOR.

Kyle Chandler

WHAT WE TRULY AND EARNESTLY ASPIRE TO BE, THAT IN SOME SENSE WE ARE.

Anna Jameson

Optimism is the faith that leads to achievement. Nothing can be done without hope and confidence.

Helen Keller

A man's reach
should exceed
his grasp,
Or what's a
heaven for?

Robert Browning

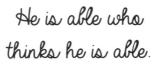

He is able who
thinks he is able.

Buddha

Live as if you were
to die tomorrow.
Learn as if you were
to live forever.

Mahatma Gandhi

Nothing is impossible to a willing heart.

John Heywood

The
BEST WAY
to make your
dreams come
true is to
WAKE UP.

Paul Valéry

BEGIN TO BE
NOW WHAT YOU WILL
BE HEREAFTER.

William James

Your imagination is your

PREVIEW

of life's coming

ATTRACTIONS.

Albert Einstein

WHAT WE PLANT
IN THE SOIL OF
CONTEMPLATION,
WE SHALL REAP
IN THE HARVEST
OF ACTION.

Meister Eckhart

A ship in harbour
is safe – but that
is not what ships
are built for.

John A. Shedd

To accomplish great things, we must not only act, but also dream; not only plan, but also believe.

Anatole France

Destiny is no matter
of chance. It is a
matter of choice.
It is not a thing
to be waited for,
it is a thing to
be achieved.

William Jennings Bryan

THE ONLY MAN WHO MAKES NO MISTAKES IS THE MAN WHO NEVER DOES ANYTHING.

Theodore Roosevelt

You can break
that big plan into
small steps and take
the first step
right away.

Indira Gandhi

Dream
LOFTY DREAMS,
and as you
DREAM,
so you shall
BECOME.

James Allen

NEVER GIVE UP, FOR
THAT IS JUST THE
PLACE AND TIME THAT
THE TIDE WILL TURN.

Harriet Beecher Stowe

If you're interested in
finding out more about our
books, find us on Facebook
at Summersdale Publishers
and follow us on Twitter
at @Summersdale.

www.summersdale.com

Image credits

pp.1–10 – © avian/Shutterstock.com; p.11 – © PinkPueblo/
Shutterstock.com; pp.13–20 – © avian/Shutterstock.com;
p.21 – © PinkPueblo/Shutterstock.com; pp.23–59 –
© avian/Shutterstock.com; p.59 – © PinkPueblo/
Shutterstock.com; pp.60–89 – © avian/Shutterstock.com;
p.90 – © PinkPueblo/Shutterstock.com; pp.91–96 –
© avian/Shutterstock.com